W9-ABL-704

ROBERT GRIFFIN III

Tammy Gagne

Mitchell Lane
PUBLISHERS

P.O. Box 196
Hockessin, Delaware 19707
Visit us on the web: www.mitchelllane.com
Comments? Email us: mitchelllane@mitchelllane.com

Printing   1   2   3   4   5   6   7   8   9

A Robbie Reader Biography

Abigail Breslin
Adrian Peterson
Albert Einstein
Albert Pujols
Aly and AJ
Andrew Luck
AnnaSophia Robb
Ashley Tisdale
Brenda Song
Brittany Murphy
Buster Posey
Charles Schulz
Chris Johnson
Cliff Lee
Dale Earnhardt Jr.
David Archuleta
Demi Lovato
Donovan McNabb

Drake Bell & Josh Peck
Dr. Seuss
Dwayne "The Rock" Johnson
Dwyane Wade
Dylan & Cole Sprouse
Emily Osment
Hilary Duff
Jamie Lynn Spears
Jennette McCurdy
Jesse McCartney
Jimmie Johnson
Joe Flacco
Jonas Brothers
Keke Palmer
Larry Fitzgerald
LeBron James
Mia Hamm
Miguiel Cabrera

Miley Cyrus
Miranda Cosgrove
Philo Farnsworth
Raven-Symoné
Robert Griffin III
Roy Halladay
Shaquille O'Neal
Story of Harley-Davidson
Sue Bird
Syd Hoff
Tiki Barber
Tim Lincecum
Tom Brady
Tony Hawk
Troy Polamalu
Victor Cruz
Victoria Justice

Library of Congress Cataloging-in-Publication Data
Gagne, Tammy.
 Robert Griffin III / by Tammy Gagne.
    pages cm. — (A robbie reader)
 Includes bibliographical references and index.
 ISBN 978-1-61228-459-0 (library bound)
 1. Griffin, Robert, III, 1990– 2. Football players—United States—Biography—Juvenile literature. 3. Quarterbacks (Football)—United States—Biography—Juvenile literature. I. Title.
 GV939.G775G34 2014
 796.332092—dc23
 [B]
                                                                                    2013023062
eBook ISBN: 9781612285177

ABOUT THE AUTHOR: Tammy Gagne is the author of numerous books for adults and children, including *Buster Posey* and *Aaron Rodgers* for Mitchell Lane Publishers. She resides in northern New England with her husband and son. One of her favorite pastimes is visiting schools to speak to kids about the writing process.

PUBLISHER'S NOTE: The following story has been thoroughly researched and to the best of our knowledge represents a true story. While every possible effort has been made to ensure accuracy, the publisher will not assume liability for damages caused by inaccuracies in the data, and makes no warranty on the accuracy of the information contained herein. This story has not been authorized or endorsed by Robert Griffin III.

TABLE OF CONTENTS

Words in **bold** type can be found in the glossary.

Robert Griffin III scored a tie-breaking touchdown in the third quarter of a game against the Dallas Cowboys on December 30, 2012. The win took place at FedEx Field in Landover, Maryland. It earned the Washington Redskins first place in the National Football Conference East division and a spot in the playoffs.

Rising to the Challenge

Robert Griffin III had a lot to be thankful for on Thanksgiving Day of 2012. He was in Dallas, Texas, a couple of hours from his childhood home, playing in a game against the Dallas Cowboys. Most **rookies** do not get the chance to start in games played on the holiday. Robert was not going to waste the important opportunity.

The Washington Redskins quarterback completed 20 of 28 passes for 311 yards and four touchdowns. Fans in the Dallas stadium chanted "RG3!" and Washington won the game with a final score of 38 to 31. People said it was one of the best Thanksgiving Day performances in NFL history. For Robert, it became one of his greatest memories of the season.

Robert reinjured his knee in a playoff game against the Seattle Seahawks on January 6, 2013. Because of the injury, Robert had to watch the end of the game from the bench. The Redskins lost with a final score of 24 to 14. Robert would have knee surgery three days later.

But Robert wasn't so lucky in early December. In a game the Redskins were losing to the Baltimore Ravens, Robert went down. His teammate, Kirk Cousins, stepped in and tied things up, forcing the game into overtime. Washington won the game with a final score of 31 to 28. But Robert had hurt his right knee badly. He returned to play two weeks later only to reinjure the knee in January. Some people thought it was the end of Robert's promising career. Once again, though, the young player appears to have beaten the odds.

Robert had surgery in January of 2013. Following the operation, Doctor James Andrews told *The Washington Post,* "We expect a full recovery and it is everybody's hope and belief that due to Robert's high motivation, he will be ready for the 2013 season."

Robert and his mother Jacqueline are very close. Here, she appears with him on the court at a basketball halftime ceremony at Baylor University, where Robert attended college.

Faster Than a Speeding Bullet

Robert Griffin III was born in Okinawa, Japan, on February 12, 1990. His parents, Robert Jr. and Jacqueline, had met many years earlier in New Orleans, Louisiana. After graduating from Kennedy High School, Robert Jr. and Jackie went their separate ways. He signed up for the United States Army. She went to college. Two years later, Jackie also joined the army. The pair met again when they were stationed together at Fort Carson in Colorado.

By the time Robert III came along, both his parents had reached the rank of **sergeant**. They also had two older children, Robert's sisters Jihan and De'Jon. The family didn't stay overseas for long after Robert's birth. They returned to the United States, living at Fort Lewis in Washington and then in New Orleans. When Robert was seven years old, they finally

Baylor Pro Day allows NFL scouts to get a look at promising young players at the university. Robert Griffin arrived at the event on March 21, 2012, with a very special cheerleader, his niece Jania Hope Moten-Griffin.

settled in Copperas Cove, Texas, near Fort Hood.

The Griffins were an active family. When they lived in the northwest, they often spent time hiking together at Mount St. Helens and Mount Rainier. They also enjoyed ice skating in Portland, Oregon. Robert III was an athletic child, taking after his father. Robert Jr. had been part of his high school basketball and track teams. When Robert III ran track, his father was his coach. A huge fan of Michael Jordan and John Elway, young Robert also played basketball, baseball, and football.

Robert grew up very close to his great-grandmother, Evelyn Thomas. Although she lived in Altadena, California, she made many trips to Texas while Robert was young. She recalls that his earliest heroes weren't athletes. "As a kid he collected action figures and would spend hours in his room alone playing with them," she told the *Los Angeles Sentinel.* "His favorite one was Superman." No one knew at this time that Robert would one day become a hero in his own right.

Arthur Jones, defensive end for the Baltimore Ravens, managed to pull Robert to the ground during a game on December 9, 2012. The Redskins nonetheless went on to win the game in overtime with a final score of 31 to 28.

On the Right Track

Robert was a talented high school athlete. While running track, he won a national championship as a **hurdler** and broke two state records. He ran the 110-meter hurdles race in 13.55 seconds and finished the 300-meter hurdles in 35.33 seconds. His time was less than a second away from the national record in the 300 meter.

Robert liked running track, but he loved playing football. By the time he was a junior, he had earned himself the position of starting quarterback on the Copperas Cove High School Bulldawgs.

In just two seasons, Robert threw for 3,300 yards, ran for 2,161 yards, and brought his team 73 total touchdowns. Jack Welch, Robert's coach with the Bulldawgs, had known all along that Robert was one to watch. "Some kids grow into their height, grow into their

Robert attended college at Baylor University because he liked the head coach there, Art Briles. Now that Robert is a professional athlete, his former coach still takes time to visit. Here, Robert and Briles talk before the Redskins game on December 30, 2012.

size," he told *The Washington Post.* "He had to grow into his talent."

When he did, the college **scouts** took notice. Some coaches thought Robert should be playing safety. Others insisted that he'd make a great receiver. Welch explained to *The Washington Post,* "Robert's his own man. He's going to do what he wants to do. If he didn't feel like doing something, he didn't do it." He told those other coaches that Robert could play either of those positions if he wanted to, "But guys," he predicted, "Robert's going to play quarterback."

Robert didn't just excel on the football field. He was also a star student. He graduated from high school early, seventh in his class, with an A average. This, combined with his athletic ability, gave him many college options. Illinois, Oregon, Stanford, Tulsa, and Washington State all wanted him. Robert liked Houston, though. Houston coach Art Briles saw Robert as a quarterback who could do great things. But when Briles decided to take the head coaching job at Baylor University, Robert followed him there instead.

Robert proved his high school coach Jack Welch right when he became a talented quarterback at Baylor University. Here he is in an NCAA college football game against Texas on December 3, 2011.

Making a Name for Himself

Robert became the starting quarterback for the Baylor Bears in the fall of 2008. He won the Big 12 **Conference's** Offensive Freshman of the Year award. He also had a **completion rate** of 60 percent for more than 2,000 yards and 15 touchdowns. Robert also picked up a new nickname: RG3. Despite his performance, Baylor finished last in the Big 12's South Division for 2008. They had company, though. They tied Texas A&M University for the spot.

Robert's second season with Baylor seemed to end even before it got going. In his third game, a play by Northwestern State

University stopped him in his tracks. The sudden move bent his right knee the wrong way. He dropped to the ground. Soon everyone started chanting Robert's name until he rose and walked slowly off the field. Because of the injury, he missed the rest of the 2009 season.

But in 2010, Robert returned to the Bears an even better player than before his

Robert performed well at Baylor's Pro Day in Waco on March 21, 2012.

injury. He led the Bears to win seven of their first nine games. The team that had tied for last in 2008 was ranked in the AP Top 25 by the middle of the season. Robert completed 304 of 454 passes for 3,501 yards. He threw for 22 touchdowns and scored another eight on the ground.

Robert and the Bears made it into the AP Top 25 again in 2011. They also won their first game ever against the Oklahoma Sooners. The year proved to be one of personal triumph for Robert as well. He won the 77th Heisman Trophy on December 10, 2011. He was the first Baylor player in history to receive the honor. He wore a striking navy blue suit to the ceremony, along with bright blue Superman socks.

It was time to follow in the footsteps of another one of his heroes. When Robert declared himself eligible for the next NFL **draft**, the Washington Redskins snatched him up with the second pick. He would now be playing for Mike Shanahan, the man who had coached John Elway to a Super Bowl win in Denver.

THE HEISMAN MEMORIAL TROPHY
PRESENTED BY
THE HEISMAN TROPHY TRUST
TO
ROBERT GRIFFIN III
BAYLOR UNIVERSITY
AS THE OUTSTANDING COLLEGE FOOTBALL PLAYER
IN THE UNITED STATES FOR
2011

Robert won the Heisman Trophy in December 2011. Here he holds the award proudly at a news conference in New York.

Mr. Griffin Goes to Washington

Art Briles was sad to see Robert leave Baylor University, but he told ESPN that it was time. "I'm excited, and I'm happy for Robert, for the way he's conducted himself for four years and the journey he has in front of him."

Robert soon realized that the beginning of his journey might be the hardest part. As he told the Associated Press, "This is the longest year of your life—for rookies, coming straight out of college, going right into combine training, pro days, minicamps, OTAs (organized team activities). It just keeps going. I'm not going to be sad or mad about it. I have a

It didn't take long for a professional team to snatch Robert up. When he declared himself eligible for the NFL draft, he was selected second overall by the Washington Redskins in the first round. It was a proud moment as he held up a Redskins jersey at Radio City Music Hall on April 26, 2012.

blessed life and I'm going to go out and make sure I continue to lead that blessed life."

Shortly after the 2012 season began, Robert was already proving that Mike Shanahan had chosen wisely. Robert was named NFL offensive rookie of the month in September. He received the honor a second time in November. In doing so he became the first player since Rams quarterback Sam Bradford

Mike Shanahan believed in Robert's abilities from the very beginning. Here the two are seen talking during the second half of a preseason game on August 25, 2012.

in 2010 to earn the title more than once in a single season.

Since the injury that ended his 2012 season early, Robert has been focused on his recovery. But it hasn't kept him from helping others when he can. In June 2013, Robert attended an event hosted by teammate Pierre

Robert enjoys working with kids. On April 25, 2012, he participated in an event for NFL Play 60 in New York. The Play 60 program teaches kids the importance of being active for at least 60 minutes each day.

Garcon to raise money for the Boys & Girls Clubs of Greater Washington. The organization helps kids in the Washington, DC, area to build confidence, develop character, and become productive, responsible adults. Guests of the fundraising party were asked to wear all white. This created a minor problem for the

After his third day of training camp on July 28, 2012, Robert was more than happy to sign some autographs for excited fans in Ashburn, Virginia.

Robert and girlfriend Rebecca attended the 2nd Annual NFL Honors on February 2, 2013, in New Orleans. Just a few months later the couple would be married.

normally colorful Robert. "This was definitely not in my closet," he told *The Washington Post* when asked about his borrowed white tuxedo. He skipped the Superman socks, but he did insist on pairing the tux with a pink shirt and sneakers.

When Robert married longtime girlfriend Rebecca Liddicoat on July 6, 2013, the bride wasn't the only one wearing white. Robert too decided to wear white from head to toe. He still managed to sneak in some color, though. His groomsmen wore bright pink vests and ties.

Even though Robert is still young, he's already made an impact both on and off the field. His coaches and teammates respect him for the role he's taken on as leader of the team. "I don't think you could find one guy in here who doesn't believe in him and believe in what he says," Redskins tight end Chris Cooley told *The Washington Post.* "I'm just totally blown away."

CHRONOLOGY

1990   Robert Griffin III is born on February 12.

1997   The Griffin family moves to Copperas Cove, Texas.

2007   Named Gatorade Texas Boys Track & Field Athlete of the Year; graduates seventh in his class from Copperas Cove High School.

2008   Enrolls in Baylor University and becomes starting quarterback for the Bears; wins NCAA Midwest Region title in 400-meter hurdles; named Big 12 Conference Offensive Freshman of the Year.

2009   Suffers first ACL injury.

2010   Leads Baylor Bears into Top 25; graduates early from Baylor University with a degree in Political Science.

2011   Begins work on his Master's degree at Baylor University; helps Baylor Bears win first game against Oklahoma Sooners; wins Heisman Trophy.

2012   Picked second in NFL draft by Washington Redskins.

2013   Injures his right knee and has surgery; marries longtime girlfriend Rebecca Liddicoat on July 6.

CAREER STATISTICS

Year	Team	PC	PA	PY	C%	PTDs	INTs	PR	RA	RY	RTDs
2008	Baylor Bears	160	267	2091	59.9	15	3	142	173	846	13
2009	Baylor Bears	45	69	481	65.2	4	0	142.9	27	77	2
2010	Baylor Bears	304	454	3501	67	22	8	144.2	149	635	8
2011	Baylor Bears	291	402	4293	72.4	37	6	189.5	179	699	10
2012	Washington Redskins	258	393	3200	65.6	20	5	102.4	120	815	7

PC = Pass Completions, PA = Pass Attemps, PY = Passing Yards, C% = Completion Percentage, PTDs = Passing Touchdowns, INTs = Interceptions, PR = Passer Rating, RA = Rushing Attempts, RY = Rushing Yards, RTDs = Rushing Touchdowns

FIND OUT MORE

Books

Elfin, David. *Washington Redskins: The Complete Illustrated History.* Minneapolis, MN: MVP Books, 2011.

Works Consulted

Associated Press. "NFL Notebook: Robert Griffin Impresses Redskins." *Tulsa World,* June 14, 2012.

Baylor Bears. "Robert Griffin III." http://www.baylorbears.com/sports/m-footbl/mtt/griffiniii_robert00.html

Collier, Jamal. "Ranking RG3's Big Game Amongst Greatest Thanksgiving Day Performances Ever." Bleacher Report, November 22, 2012.

ESPN.com News Services. "Robert Griffin III Headed to NFL." January 12, 2012. http://espn.go.com/nfl/draft2012/story/_/id/7451661/heisman-trophy-winner-robert-griffin-iii-declares-nfl-draft

Jackie Griffin. "Raising Robert Griffin III." http://www.rg3mom.com

Jones, Mike. "Robert Griffin III Named NFL Rookie of the Month." *The Washington Post,* November 29, 2012.

FIND OUT MORE

Jones, Mike. "Robert Griffin III's ACL Reconstructed Again, LCL Repaired, Surgeon Says." *The Washington Post,* January 9, 2013.

Kogod, Sarah. "Redskins Dress in All White for Pierre Garcon's Charity Event." *The Washington Post,* June 7, 2013.

Lewis, Jason. "It's A Family Affair." *Los Angeles Sentinel,* December 17, 2011.

Lewis, Ted. "NFL Draft: Robert Griffin III and Family Ties from New Orleans Are Poised to Celebrate." *The Times-Picayune,* April 26, 2012.

Maese, Rick. "Sky's the Limit for Griffin." *The Washington Post,* April 22, 2012.

The Monitor. "Baylor QB Griffin Out for Season." September 27, 2009.

Reid, Jason. "Robert Griffin III Demonstrates Leadership Qualities Rare for a Rookie of Any Sport." *The Washington Post,* November 28, 2012.

Whiteside, Kelly. "Baylor Quarterback Robert Griffin III Captures Heisman Trophy." *USA Today,* December 11, 2011.

On the Internet

BaylorBears.com: "Robert Griffin III"
http://bu-rg3.com

NFL.com: "RG3 Zone"
http://www.nfl.com/qs/rg3zone/index.jsp

Sports Illustrated Kids
http://www.sikids.com

Washington Redskins Kids Club
http://www.redskinskidsclub.com

GLOSSARY

completion rate (kuhm-PLEE-shuhn REYT)–the percentage of a quarterback's passes that are caught.

conference (KON-fur-uhnss)–a group of school or professional athletic teams that play against each other regularly.

draft (DRAFT)–an event in which professional teams choose new players.

hurdle (HUR-dl)–a barrier over which runners jump in certain races.

rookie (ROOK-ee)–an athlete playing in his or her first season as a professional.

sergeant (SAHR-juhnt)–an army officer with a rank above that of specialist and corporal, but below staff sergeant.

scout (SKOUT)–a person whose job is to look for talented young athletes for a particular sports team.

INDEX

DISCARD